D1272408

Moon Landing

written by
Joe Dunn

illustrated by
Joseph Wight, Rod Espinosa & Lee Duhig

Charles County Public Library
Potomac Branch
301-375-7375
www.ccplonline.org

magic
wagon

visit us at
www.abdopublishing.com

Published by Magic Wagon, a division of the ABDO Publishing Group, 8000 West 78th Street, Edina, Minnesota 55439. Copyright © 2008 by Abdo Consulting Group, Inc. International copyrights reserved in all countries. All rights reserved. No part of this book may be reproduced in any form without written permission from the publisher. Graphic Planet™ is a trademark and logo of Magic Wagon.

Printed in the United States.

Written by Joe Dunn
Illustrated by Joseph Wight, Rod Espinosa and Lee Duhig
Colored by Joseph Wight and GURU-eFX
Lettered by Joseph Wight
Edited by Stephanie Hedlund
Interior layout and design by Antarctic Press
Cover art by Rod Espinosa
Cover design by Neil Klinepier

Library of Congress Cataloging-in-Publication Data

Dunn, Joeming W.
    Moon Landing / Joe Dunn ; illustrated by Joseph Wight, Rod Espinosa and Lee Duhig.
    p. cm. -- (Graphic history)
    Includes index.
    ISBN 978-1-60270-078-9
    1. Project Apollo (U.S.)--Comic books, strips, etc.--Juvenile literature. 2. Space flight to the moon--Comic books, strips, etc.--Juvenile literature. 3. Astronautics--United States--History--Comic books, strips, etc.--Juvenile literature. I. Wight, Joseph, ill. II. Espinosa, Rod, ill. III. Duhig, Lee, ill. IV. Title.

TL789.8.U6A5326 2008
629.45'4--dc22

                                      2007006443

TABLE of CONTENTS

Timeline

October 4, 1957 - The Soviet Union launched *Sputnik I.*

November 3, 1957 - *Sputnik II* carried a dog named Laika into space.

January 3, 1958 - The United States launched *Explorer 1* into orbit.

April 9, 1959 - NASA introduced the first seven U.S. astronauts.

April 12, 1961 - Cosmonaut Yury Gagarin from the Soviet Union was the first human in space.

May 2, 1961 - Alan Shepard became the first American in space.

May 25, 1961 - President John F. Kennedy set a goal to land on the moon by the end of the decade.

February 20, 1962 - John Glenn became the first American to orbit Earth.

March 23, 1965 - *Gemini 3* was launched. This began the Gemini flights.

January 27, 1967 - Three Apollo astronauts, Gus Grissom, Edward White II and Roger Chaffee, died in their capsule.

December 21 to 27, 1968 - *Apollo 8* completed the first manned orbit of the moon.

July 11, 1969 - *Apollo 11* launched.

July 20, 1969 - Astronauts Neil Armstrong and Buzz Aldrin became the first men on the moon.

July 24, 1969 - *Apollo 11* returned to Earth.

"I BELIEVE THAT THIS NATION SHOULD
COMMIT ITSELF TO ACHIEVING THE GOAL,
BEFORE THE DECADE IS OUT, OF
LANDING A MAN ON THE MOON AND
RETURNING HIM SAFELY TO EARTH."

- JOHN F. KENNEDY

Chapter 1 — Dreams about the Moon

THE WORLD HAS ALWAYS BEEN FASCINATED WITH THE MOON.

SINCE ANCIENT TIMES, THE MOON HAS BEEN AN OBJECT OF WORSHIP, SOMETIMES LOOKED UPON AS A GOD.

ONE OF THE FIRST WRITTEN STORIES ABOUT TRAVELING TO THE MOON WAS BY LUCIAN OF SAMOSATA.

LUCIAN WAS A GREEK WRITER WHO WROTE ABOUT A SAILING SHIP RIDING THE CURRENTS TO THE MOON.

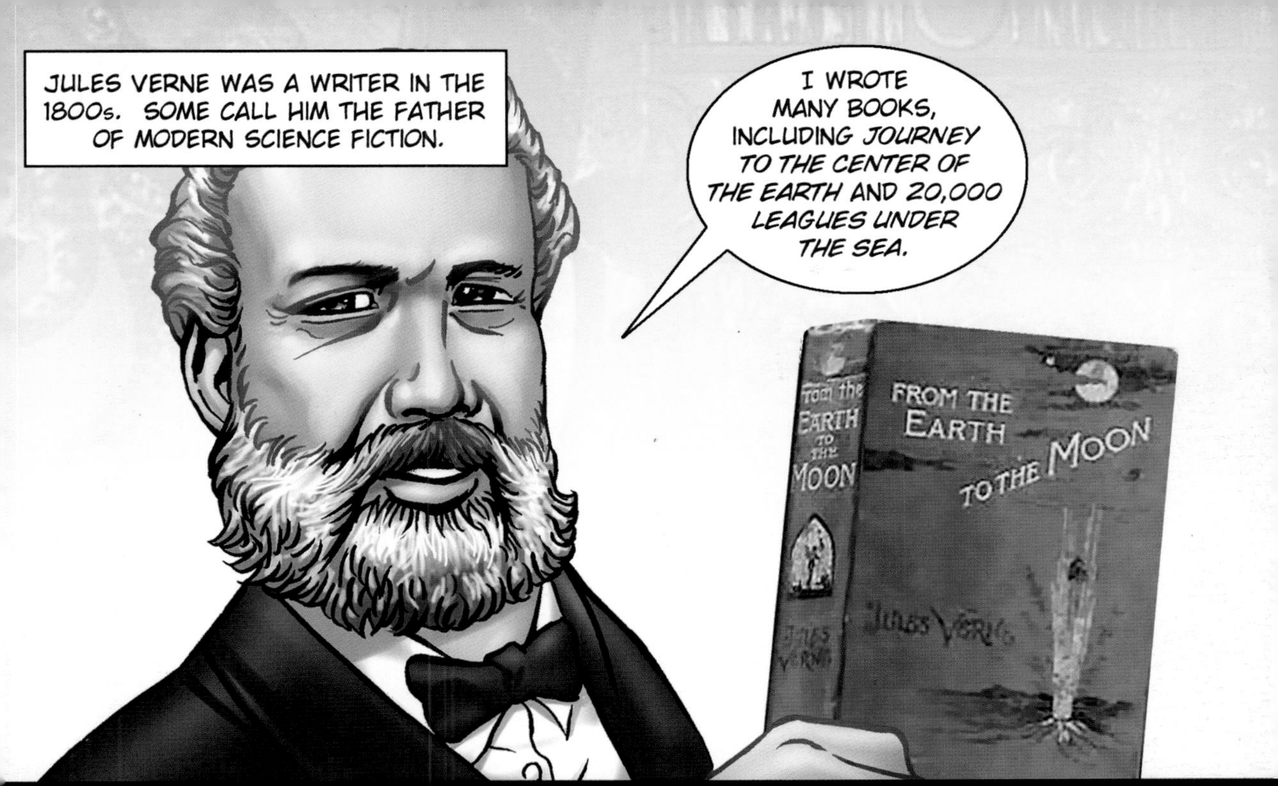
JULES VERNE WAS A WRITER IN THE 1800s. SOME CALL HIM THE FATHER OF MODERN SCIENCE FICTION.
I WROTE MANY BOOKS, INCLUDING *JOURNEY TO THE CENTER OF THE EARTH* AND *20,000 LEAGUES UNDER THE SEA.*
FROM THE EARTH TO THE MOON
JULES VERNE

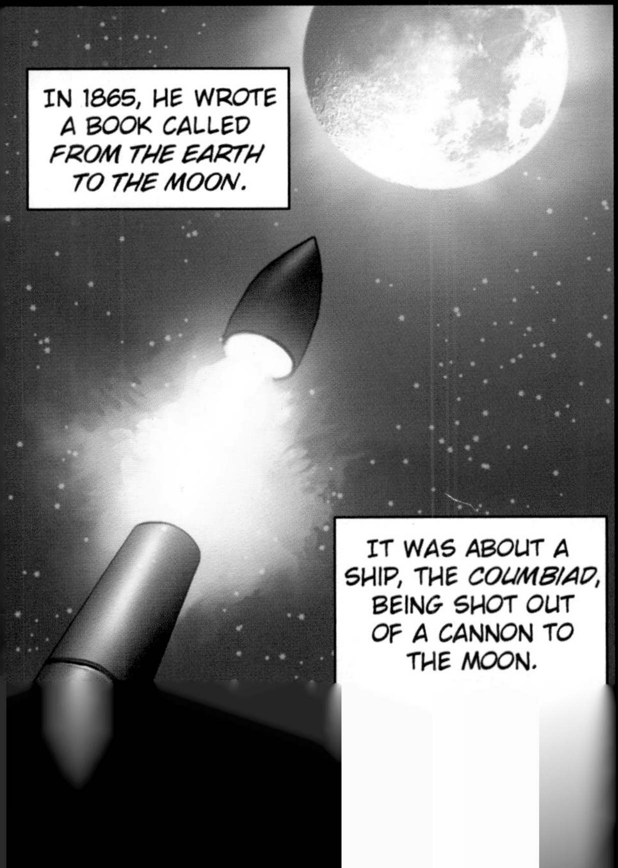
IN 1865, HE WROTE A BOOK CALLED *FROM THE EARTH TO THE MOON*.
IT WAS ABOUT A SHIP, THE *COUMBIAD*, BEING SHOT OUT OF A CANNON TO THE MOON.

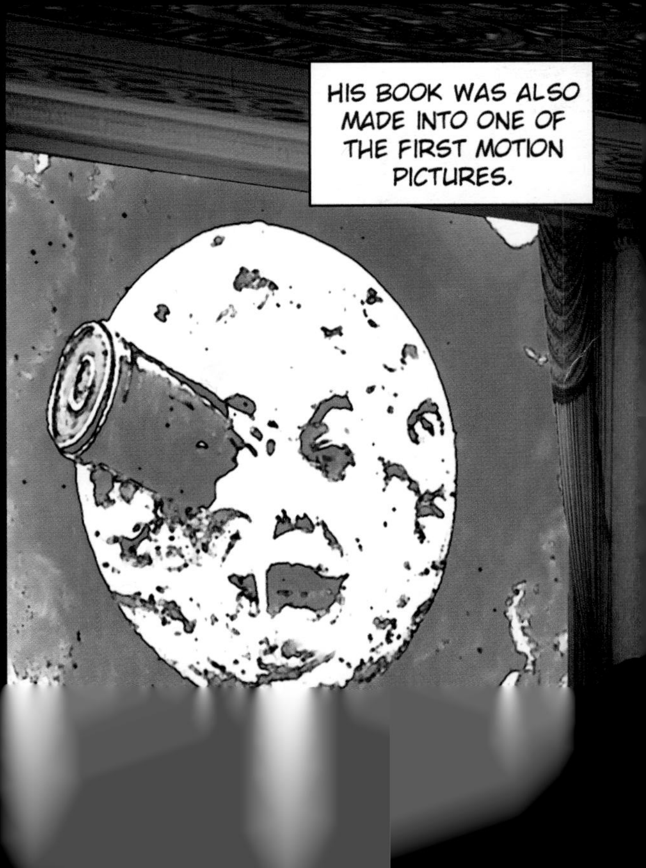
HIS BOOK WAS ALSO MADE INTO ONE OF THE FIRST MOTION PICTURES.

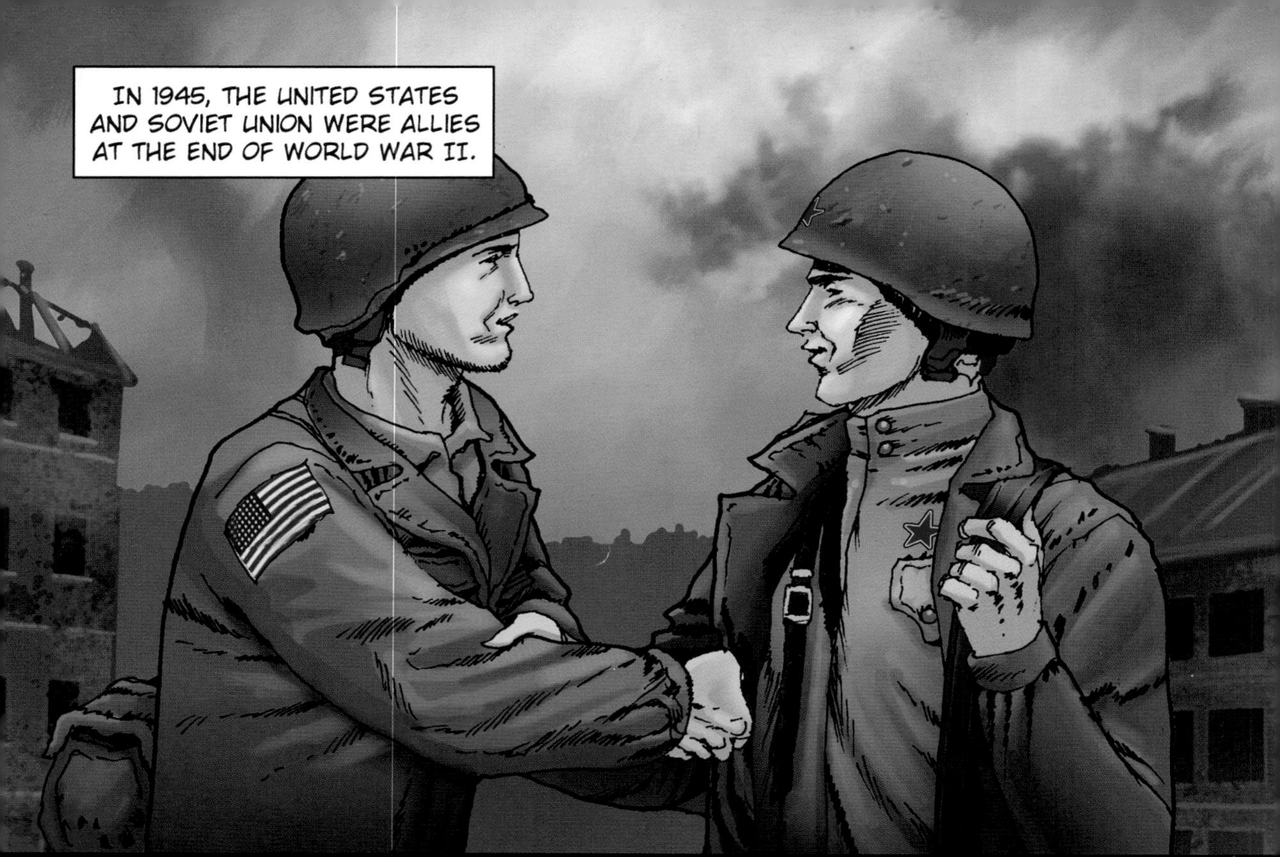
IN 1945, THE UNITED STATES AND SOVIET UNION WERE ALLIES AT THE END OF WORLD WAR II.

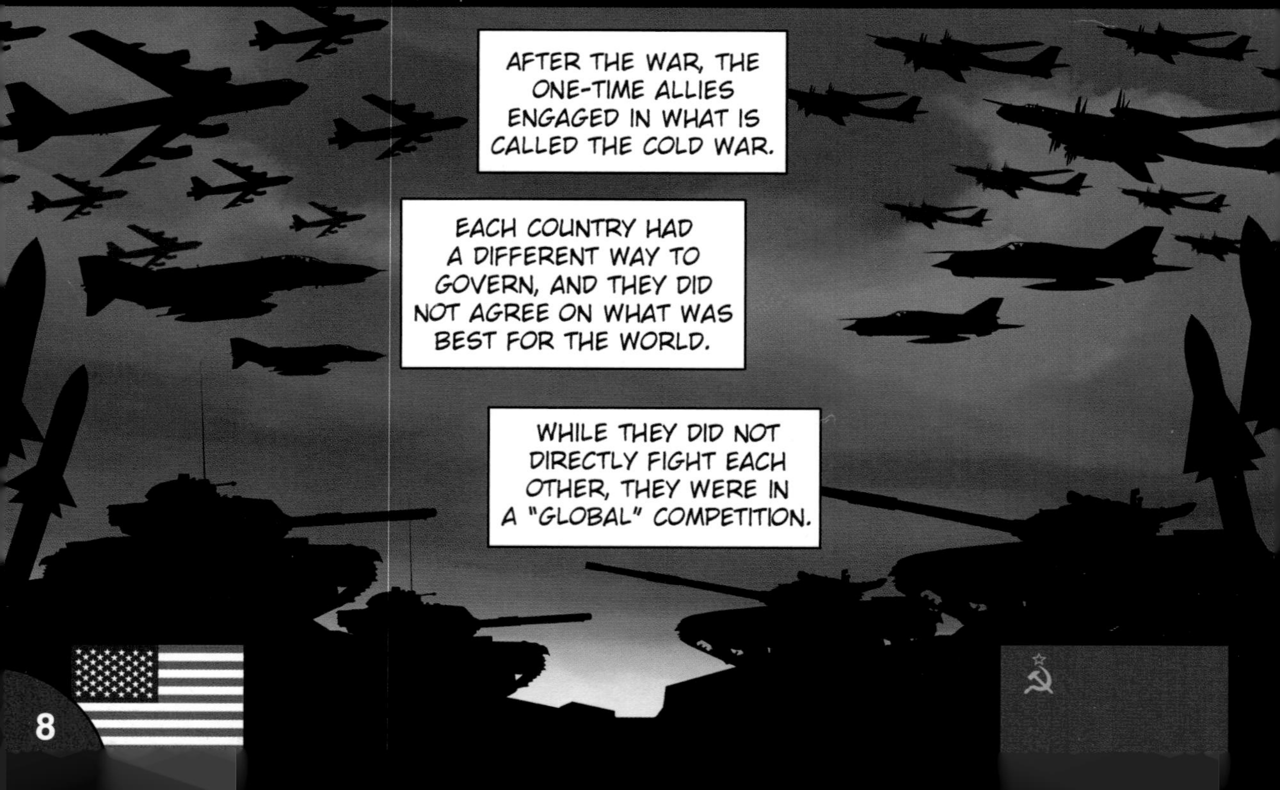
AFTER THE WAR, THE ONE-TIME ALLIES ENGAGED IN WHAT IS CALLED THE COLD WAR.
EACH COUNTRY HAD A DIFFERENT WAY TO GOVERN, AND THEY DID NOT AGREE ON WHAT WAS BEST FOR THE WORLD.
WHILE THEY DID NOT DIRECTLY FIGHT EACH OTHER, THEY WERE IN A "GLOBAL" COMPETITION.

THE COMPETITION INCLUDED WHO COULD GET INTO SPACE FIRST.

ON OCTOBER 4, 1957, THE SOVIET UNION LAUNCHED THE FIRST SPACE SATELLITE. IT WAS CALLED *SPUTNIK I.*

IT COULD CIRCLE EARTH IN ONE AND A HALF HOURS.

ALL THE SATELLITE COULD DO WAS SEND A BEEPING SIGNAL, WHICH WAS MONITORED ON THE GROUND.

I CAN HEAR IT... I CAN HEAR IT!

IT ORBITED FOR 92 DAYS BEFORE IT BURNED UP IN EARTH'S ATMOSPHERE.

WITH THE LAUNCH OF *SPUTNIK*, MANY AMERICANS BECAME WORRIED THAT THE SOVIETS HAD A WAY TO LAUNCH BOMBS TO ATTACK THE UNITED STATES.

THIS STARTED THE SPACE RACE, IN WHICH BOTH SIDES WORKED FRANTICALLY TO ACHIEVE THE NEXT SPACE LAUNCH.

ONE MONTH AFTER *SPUTNIK I*, THE SOVIET UNION LAUNCHED *SPUTNIK 2*.

THIS SATELLITE WAS SIX TIMES BIGGER THAN THE FIRST, AND IT CARRIED A SMALL DOG NAMED LAIKA.

LAIKA WOULD BE THE FIRST LIVING BEING TO ORBIT THE EARTH.

UNFORTUNATELY, LAIKA DID NOT SURVIVE THE MISSION.

THE U.S. SPACE PROGRAM, THE NATIONAL AERONAUTICS AND SPACE ADMINISTRATION (NASA), ATTEMPTED TO LAUNCH ITS FIRST SATELLITE ON DECEMBER 6, 1957.

IT FELL AND EXPLODED ON THE LAUNCHPAD AFTER LIFTING OFF A FEW INCHES.

IN EARLY 1958, THE UNITED STATES SUCCESSFULLY LAUNCHED THE *EXPLORER I* SATELLITE.

THE EXPLORER SATELLITES WERE THE FIRST TO TAKE PICTURES OF EARTH'S SURFACE FROM SPACE.

ON APRIL 12, 1961, THE SOVIET UNION SENT COSMONAUT YURY GAGARIN INTO ORBIT AROUND EARTH. HE BECAME THE FIRST PERSON TO DO SO.

THE UNITED STATES SENT ASTRONAUT ALAN SHEPARD INTO SPACE LESS THAN A MONTH LATER. HE TRAVELED ON *FREEDOM 7*, A MERCURY SPACECRAFT.

"WHAT A BEAUTIFUL VIEW."

WHILE HE DID NOT ORBIT EARTH, THE ACCOMPLISHMENT SHOWED THAT BOTH COUNTRIES COULD SEND SOMEONE INTO SPACE.

SOON AFTER ALAN SHEPARD'S TRIP, PRESIDENT JOHN F. KENNEDY MADE A COMMITMENT TO LAND ON THE MOON BY THE END OF THE DECADE.

THIS NATION SHOULD COMMIT ITSELF TO ACHIEVING THE GOAL, BEFORE THIS DECADE IS OUT, OF LANDING A MAN ON THE MOON AND RETURNING HIM SAFELY TO THE EARTH.

NO SINGLE SPACE PROJECT IN THIS PERIOD WILL BE MORE IMPRESSIVE TO MANKIND, OR MORE IMPORTANT FOR THE LONG-RANGE EXPLORATION OF SPACE; AND NONE WILL BE SO DIFFICULT OR EXPENSIVE TO ACCOMPLISH.

TO ACCOMPLISH THIS GOAL, MANY STEPS HAD TO BE TAKEN IN PREPARATION.

THE FIRST AMERICAN TO ORBIT EARTH WAS ASTRONAUT JOHN GLENN. HE WENT AROUND 3 TIMES.

WHEN HE SAW THE SUNSET FROM SPACE, HE SAID, "THIS MOMENT OF TWILIGHT IS SIMPLY BEAUTIFUL. THE SKY IN SPACE IS VERY BLACK, WITH A THIN BAND OF BLUE ALONG THE HORIZON."

SCIENTISTS STUDIED THE MOON FROM A DISTANCE, BUT WE STILL DID NOT KNOW MUCH ABOUT THE ORB.

OVER THE NEXT SEVERAL YEARS, NASA SENT PROBES AND SPACECRAFT TO STUDY THE COMPOSITION AND STRUCTURE OF THE MOON, AS WELL AS TO TAKE PHOTOGRAPHS.

ALL OF THIS INFORMATION HELPED SCIENTISTS PICK THE BEST LANDING SPOT FOR THE ASTRONAUTS.

BEFORE THE LAUNCH TO THE MOON, ASTRONAUTS HAD TO PREPARE FOR WORKING IN SPACE.

SCOTT CARPENTER, GORDON COOPER, JOHN GLENN, GUS GRISSOM, WALLY SCHIRRA, ALAN SHEPARD, AND DEKE SLAYTON WERE KNOWN AS THE MERCURY SEVEN.

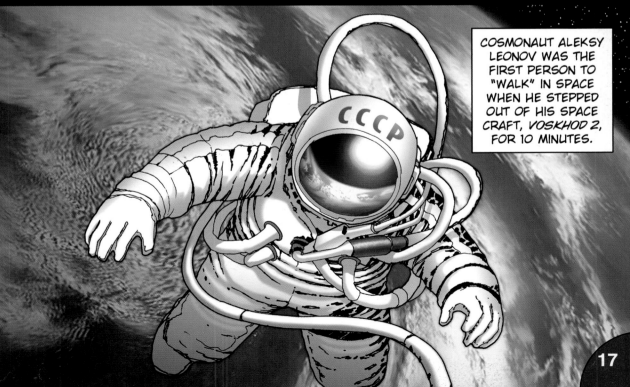

COSMONAUT ALEKSY LEONOV WAS THE FIRST PERSON TO "WALK" IN SPACE WHEN HE STEPPED OUT OF HIS SPACE CRAFT, VOSKHOD 2, FOR 10 MINUTES.

SOON AFTERWARD, EDWARD WHITE II BECAME THE FIRST AMERICAN TO WALK INTO SPACE.

NASA DEVELOPED THE GEMINI PROGRAM TO TRAIN THE ASTRONAUTS. IT TAUGHT SKILLS THAT WOULD BE NECESSARY FOR TRAVELING TO THE MOON, INCLUDING MANEUVERING AND DOCKING.

Chapter 4 Gemini Program

THEIR MISSIONS WERE VERY DANGEROUS. ONE ALMOST ENDED IN DISASTER AS THE DOCKED SHIPS SPUN OUT OF CONTROL.

FORTUNATELY, THE ASTRONAUTS REGAINED CONTROL OF THE SHIP.

WHEN THE GEMINI PROGRAM FINISHED, THE ASTRONAUTS HAD SPENT A COMBINED 2,000 HOURS IN SPACE.

GEMINI 7 STAYED IN ORBIT 14 DAYS, WHICH PROVED A TRIP TO THE MOON WAS POSSIBLE.

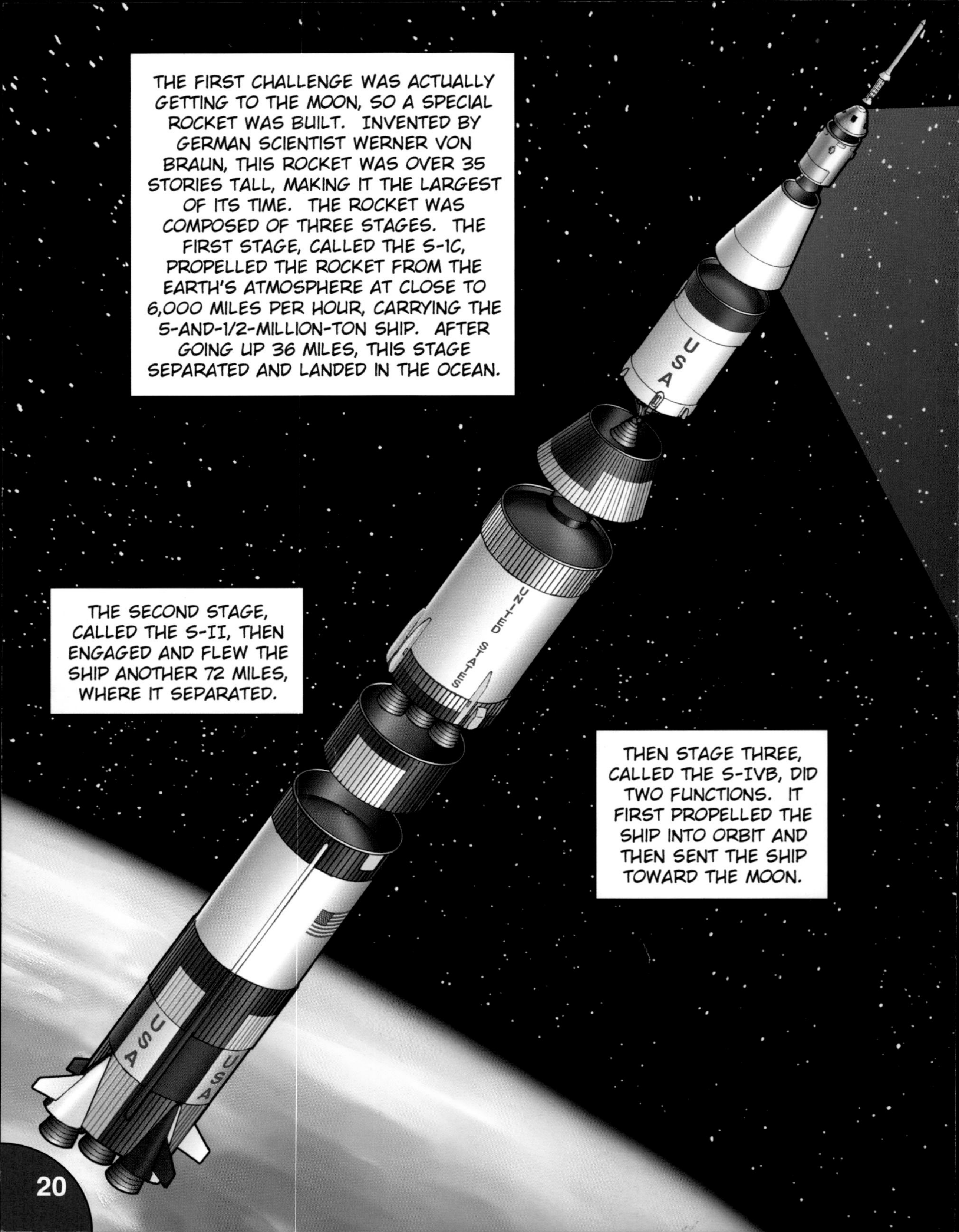
THE FIRST CHALLENGE WAS ACTUALLY GETTING TO THE MOON, SO A SPECIAL ROCKET WAS BUILT. INVENTED BY GERMAN SCIENTIST WERNER VON BRAUN, THIS ROCKET WAS OVER 35 STORIES TALL, MAKING IT THE LARGEST OF ITS TIME. THE ROCKET WAS COMPOSED OF THREE STAGES. THE FIRST STAGE, CALLED THE S-1C, PROPELLED THE ROCKET FROM THE EARTH'S ATMOSPHERE AT CLOSE TO 6,000 MILES PER HOUR, CARRYING THE 5-AND-1/2-MILLION-TON SHIP. AFTER GOING UP 36 MILES, THIS STAGE SEPARATED AND LANDED IN THE OCEAN.
USA
UNITED STATES
THE SECOND STAGE, CALLED THE S-II, THEN ENGAGED AND FLEW THE SHIP ANOTHER 72 MILES, WHERE IT SEPARATED.
THEN STAGE THREE, CALLED THE S-IVB, DID TWO FUNCTIONS. IT FIRST PROPELLED THE SHIP INTO ORBIT AND THEN SENT THE SHIP TOWARD THE MOON.
USA
USA

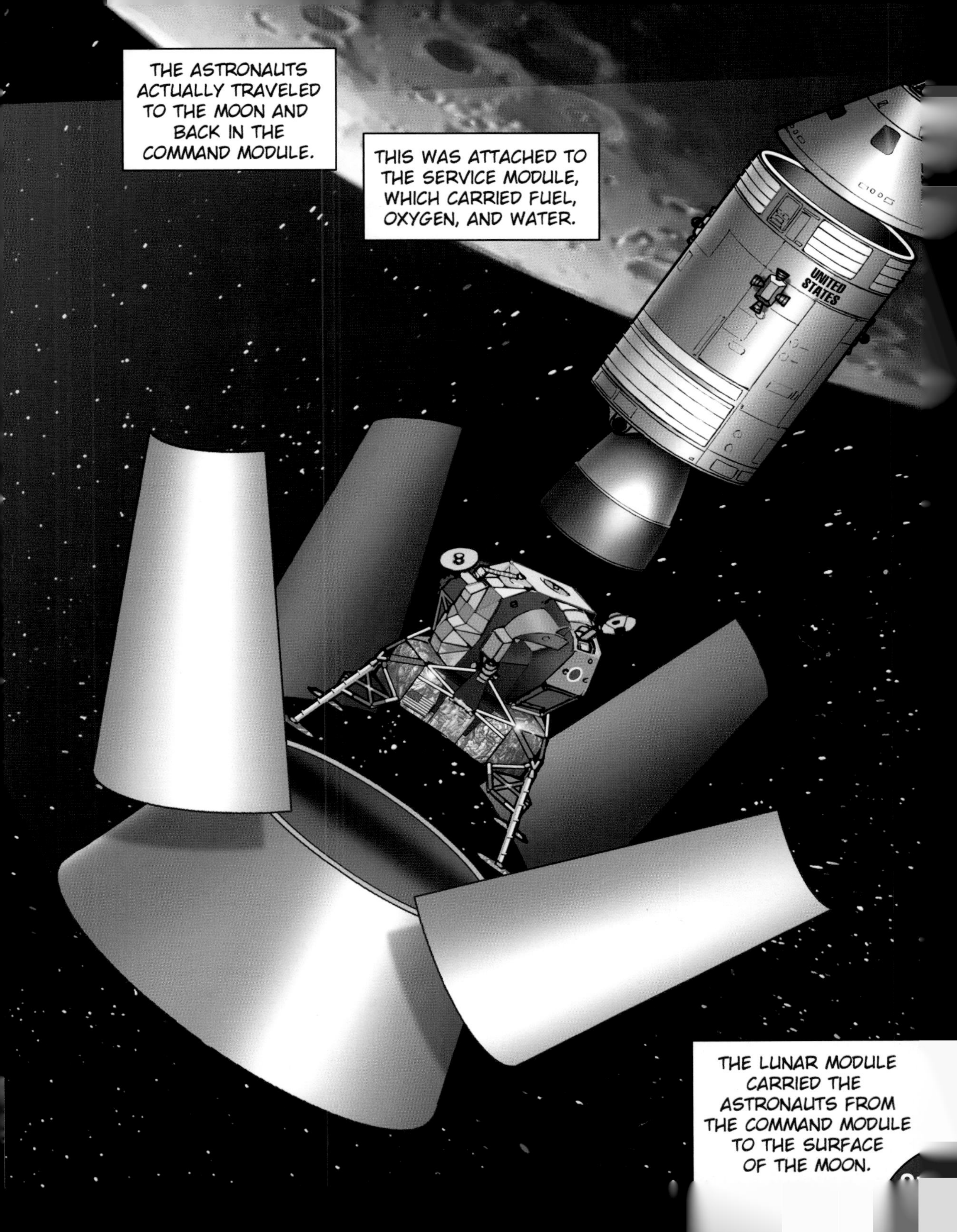
THE ASTRONAUTS ACTUALLY TRAVELED TO THE MOON AND BACK IN THE COMMAND MODULE.
THIS WAS ATTACHED TO THE SERVICE MODULE, WHICH CARRIED FUEL, OXYGEN, AND WATER.
UNITED STATES
THE LUNAR MODULE CARRIED THE ASTRONAUTS FROM THE COMMAND MODULE TO THE SURFACE OF THE MOON.

NASA STARTED THE APOLLO MISSIONS TO PREPARE FOR THE MOON LANDING.

DISASTER STRUCK EVEN BEFORE THE FIRST LAUNCH.

DURING A TEST, A FIRE IN THE COMMAND MODULE KILLED THREE ASTRONAUTS: VIRGIL "GUS" GRISSOM, ROGER CHAFFEE, AND EDWARD WHITE II.

DESPITE THE TRAGEDY, THE APOLLO MISSIONS PROVED SUCCESSFUL. APOLLO 8 WAS THE FIRST TO ORBIT THE MOON WITH ASTRONAUTS FRANK BORMAN, WILLIAM ANDERS, AND JAMES LOVELL. THEY ORBITED TEN TIMES BUT DID NOT LAND ON THE MOON.

ON JULY 16, 1969, THE UNITED STATES LAUNCHED *APOLLO 11*.

THIS MISSION WOULD SEND THE CREW TO LAND ON THE MOON.

THE ASTRONAUTS ABOARD WERE NEIL ARMSTRONG, BUZZ ALDRIN, AND MICHAEL COLLINS.

THEY TRAVELED TO THE MOON WITHOUT ANY DIFFICULTIES AND RESTED INTO ORBIT.

THE LUNAR MODULE, CALLED *EAGLE*, SEPARATED FROM THE COMMAND MODULE ON JULY 20. ASTRONAUTS ARMSTRONG AND ALDRIN WERE IN IT. ASTRONAUT COLLINS REMAINED IN THE COMMAND MODULE TO KEEP IT IN ORBIT.

THE LUNAR MODULE SLOWLY DESCENDED ONTO THE MOON. THEIR TARGET WAS THE SEA OF TRANQUILITY.

THE LUNAR MODULE LANDED SAFELY ON THE MOON.

THE *EAGLE* HAS LANDED.

THAT'S ONE SMALL STEP FOR A MAN, ONE GIANT LEAP FOR MANKIND.

Chapter 6 First Man on the Moon

ALDRIN AND ARMSTRONG SPENT 2 HOURS AND 21 MINUTES WALKING ON THE MOON.

THEY COLLECTED MOON ROCKS AND SAMPLES AND TOOK PICTURES.

AFTER SPENDING 22 HOURS ON THE MOON, THE LUNAR MODULE LIFTED OFF TO DOCK WITH THE COMMAND MODULE FOR THE TRIP BACK TO EARTH.

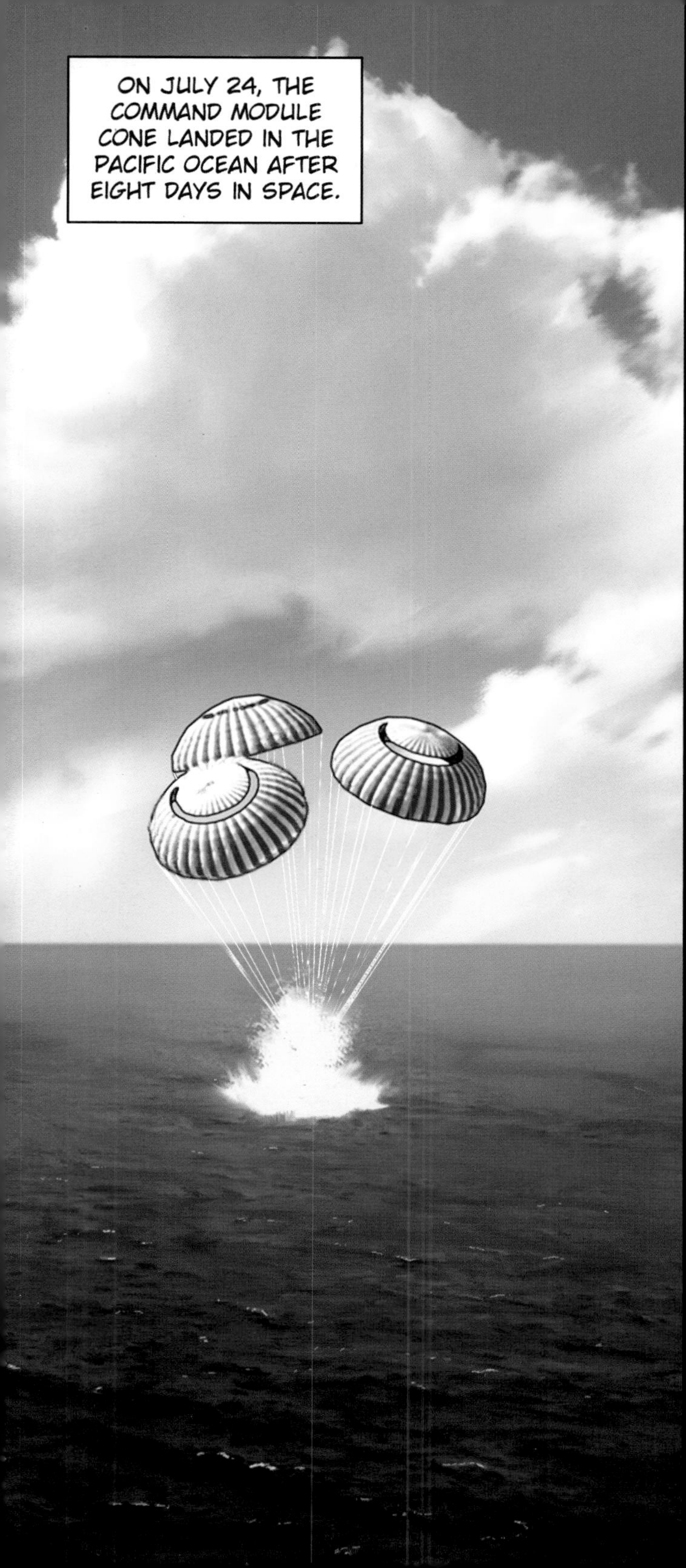
ON JULY 24, THE COMMAND MODULE CONE LANDED IN THE PACIFIC OCEAN AFTER EIGHT DAYS IN SPACE.

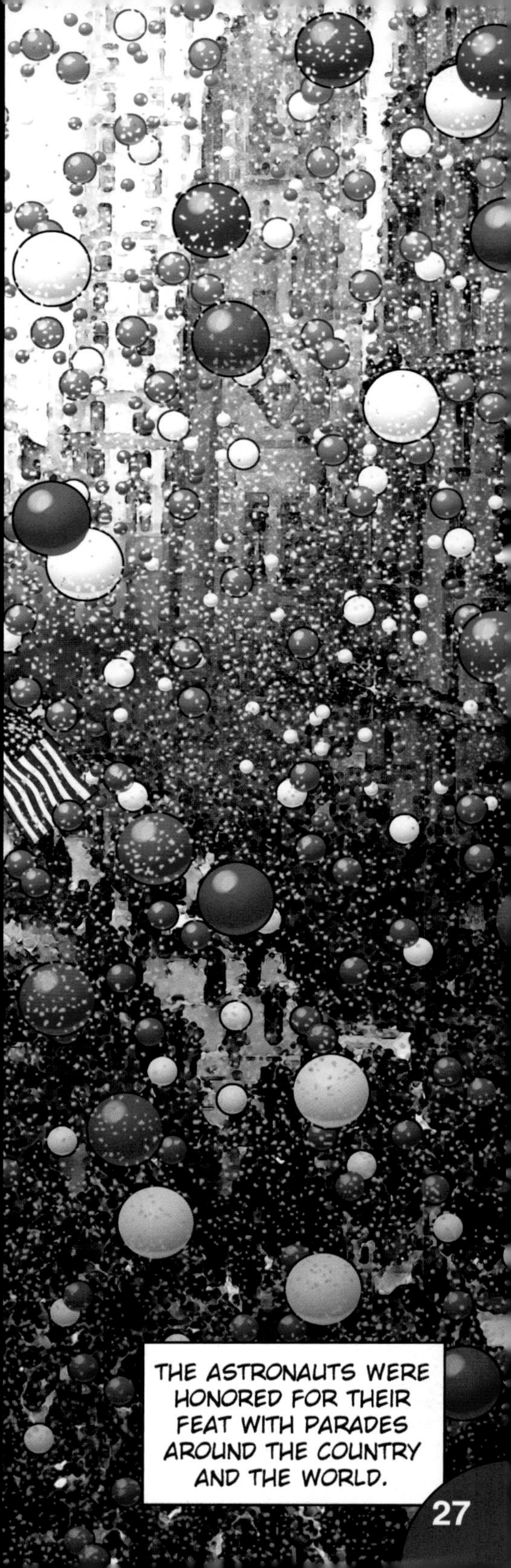
THE ASTRONAUTS WERE HONORED FOR THEIR FEAT WITH PARADES AROUND THE COUNTRY AND THE WORLD.

THE MOON LANDING SPARKED THE AGE OF SPACE EXPLORATION, TO GO TO THE MOON AND BEYOND.

Explorer Missions

Explorer 1: January 31, 1958. First satellite sent into space.
Explorer 2: March 5, 1958. Fourth rocket stage failed to ignite.
Explorer 3: March 26, 1958.
Explorer 4: July 26, 1958. Operated until October 6, 1958.
Explorer 5: August 24, 1958. Failed when booster collided with second
rocket stage.

Gemini Missions

Gemini III: March 23, 1965. First manned Gemini flight, made three
orbits.
Gemini IV: June 3-7, 1965. First American extravehicular activity (EVA),
White's 22-minute "space walk."
Gemini V: August 21-29, 1965. Guidance and navigation systems
evaluated for future missions.
Gemini VII: December 4-18, 1965. Helped determine if humans could
live in space for 14 days.
Gemini VIII: March 16, 1966. First docking with another space vehicle.

Apollo Missions

Apollo 7: October 11, 1968. First Apollo mission to fly, made 163 orbits.
Apollo 8: December 21, 1968. First occupied launch of Saturn V rocket.
Apollo 9: March 3, 1969. First human test of lunar module.
Apollo 10: May 18, 1989. Orbited the moon.
Apollo 11: July 16, 1969. First to land on the moon. Made it with 30
seconds of fuel remaining. Astronauts took core samples and
planted an American flag.

Apollo Rocket Diagram

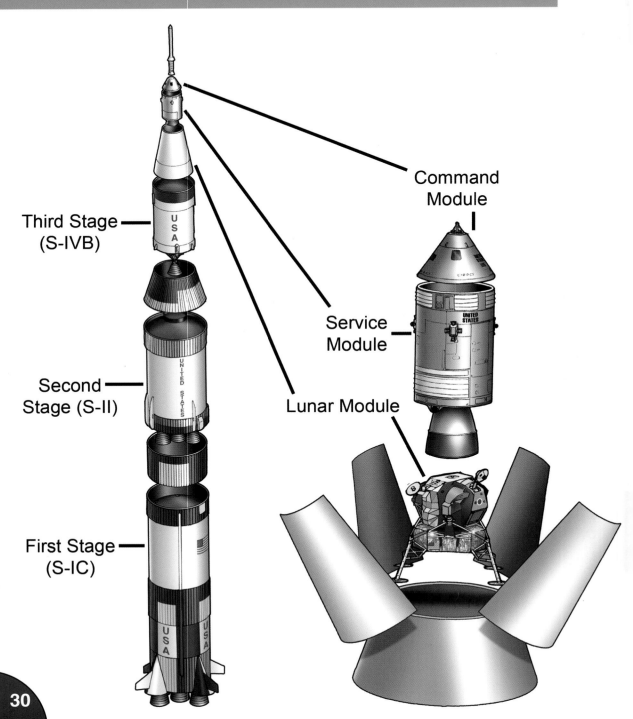

Third Stage
(S-IVB)

Second
Stage (S-II)

First Stage
(S-IC)

Command
Module

Service
Module

Lunar Module

Glossary

allies - people or countries that agree to help each other in times of need. During World War II, Great Britain, France, the United States, and the Soviet Union were called the Allies.

Cold War - a period of tension and hostility between the United States and its allies and the Soviet Union and its allies after World War II.

cosmonaut - an astronaut from Russia.

dock - to join two spacecraft while in space.

World War II - from 1939 to 1945, fought in Europe, Asia, and Africa. Great Britain, France, the United States, the Soviet Union, and their allies were on one side. Germany, Italy, Japan, and their allies were on the other side. The war began when Germany invaded Poland. The United States entered the war in 1941 after Japan bombed Pearl Harbor, Hawaii.

Web Sites

To learn more about the moon landing, visit ABDO Publishing Company on the World Wide Web at **www.abdopublishing.com.** Web sites about the moon landing are featured on our Book Links page. These links are routinely monitored and updated to provide the most current information available.

Index